MW00564907

CHARLIE PARKER OM

Transposed for B Flat Instruments • Transcribed Exactly From His Recorded Solos
(Tenor and Soprano Sax, Trumpet and Clarinet)

CONTENTS

INTRODUCTION

The solos in this book represent a cross section of the music of Charlie Parker. In presenting these solos, we hope to bring musicians closer to the true genius of "Bird".

These solos are in Bb key, transposed to sound in unison with the original solos in Eb key. For Bb saxophone a few of the lowest notes are out of range. Playing 8va a note or a phrase or even a whole page, at the discretion of the player, will provide an artistic challenge.

Most Jazz musicians have learned to play by listening to records and imitating the notes, articulations, vibrato, etc. of the masters. We encourage you to play these with the actual recording. Listen to the record first, then play through the solo slowly, gradually increasing the speed until you are at the recorded tempo Bird played it. I don't feel the idea is to try to play the solos exactly as Bird did, but rather to find phrases, articulations, scoops, turns, etc. that you feel you would like to incorporate into your own playing. By being able to see and play the actual notes, it should help speed up the learning process. Many players play like Bird but retain their own personality.

Practice with a metronome. Each day try to increase the tempo a little, all the while retaining the inflections, articulations, etc. that you would use at the slower tempo. Try practicing some of these solos with the Aebersold Play A Long records. Take a slow blues solo in F and play it with one of the records in the series that has a slow F blues, then move to a record that has a faster F blues. It is fun to work towards playing the solos with Bird along with the actual Parker recorded version.

Blues make up the largest portion of this book. Rhythm changes come next. Some compositions have the two versions recorded by Parker in separate solos. When a measure occurs without a chord symbol above it, the chord is the same as the measure preceeding it.

Most players like to analyze solos in order to find out what the musician is doing. Our ears cannot always HEAR what is happening so we slow the music down, transcribe it, analyze it, practice the licks, patterns and phrases we like best, and end up playing them in our own way on our instruments. We have put chord symbols over most all bars to enable you to analyze the notes in relation to the chord. Remember, each chord symbol represents a series of tones called a scale. Older musicians used to improvise mainly on chord tones; Charlie Parker was one of the first to broaden that to include scales **and** substitute scales. For information on scale substitution refer to the Scale Syllabus chart.* Bird loved to use the b9 over the Dom. 7th chord/scale. The Blues scale and its accompanying licks was an important part of his music, even when playing songs other than blues! When you find licks or patterns that you enjoy, practice them in several keys so the melodic phrase becomes a part of you. It should become automatic in order to really be useable in a playing situation.

Only a minimum of articulations have been put in this book. We feel that jazz, being an aural art form, is often times best imitated by listening over and over, and then playing the notes the way you hear it on the record. This might seem like the long way to do it, but experience has proven reliable. After all, who would object to listening anyway? Listening is what music is all about.

The records from which these solos are taken are listed at the top of each solo page. They are contained in approximately eight records (some are two record sets) and most all are still available. The two record sets are a bargain!

We hope you have as much enjoyment with this book as we have had putting it together.

Jamey Aebersold

* For SCALE SYLLABUS, see page 143

iv

Confirmation

By Charlie Parker

VERVE 8005

♩=208
(4-bar Intro)

TURN PAGE

W.W.

4

Moose The Mooche

By Charlie Parker

C. PARKER 407

Ornithology

By Charlie Parker and Benny Harris

'BIRD SYMBOLS'
C. PARKER 407

6

Yardbird Suite

By Charlie Parker

'BIRD SYMBOLS'
C. PARKER 407

Anthropology

By Charlie Parker and John 'Dizzy' Gillespie

COLUMBIA 34831

(Turn Page)

Dewey Square

By Charlie Parker

JAZZ GREATS JG-617/BLUE RIBBON 8011

Scrapple From The Apple

By Charlie Parker

BLUE RIBBON 8011/UP FRONT 171/CHARLIE PARKER RECORDS 407/SAVOY 1108

Blues For Alice

By Charlie Parker

VERVE 8010/VERVE 2515

K.C. Blues

By Charlie Parker

VERVE 8840/VERVE 8010/MGM 4949/VERVE 2515

THE PROFESSIONAL ARRANGER COMPOSER

(BOOK ONE)

By Russell Garcia

- Best selling text book used by leading universities.

- Basis for course in Practical Arranging and Composing in the professional field. For the advanced arranger.

- Endorsed by leading music educators and composers and arrangers.

AND NOW!

THE PROFESSIONAL ARRANGER COMPOSER

(BOOK TWO)

By Russell Garcia

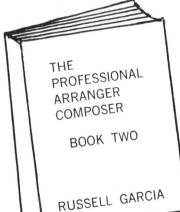

- Discusses contemporary trends in Jazz, Pop and "Modern Classical" Techniques. New scales, chords, progressions, free improvisation, vocal effects, using tone rows in practical music, etc.

- Contains a record of many of the 169 examples and the recording of a complete score of an exciting contemporary composition by Garcia. (Musicians used are the top instrumentalists on the West Coast).

The both books complement each other!
You need both books for a complete course!

CRITERION MUSIC CORPORATION
6124 Selma Avenue, Hollywood, 90028 Calif.

Celerity

By Charlie Parker

VERVE 8002/VERVE 2512

Au Privave
(No. 1)

By Charlie Parker

VERVE 8010/MGM 4949/VERVE 2515

≣ **STAGE DANCE BAND** ≣

Arranged by Frank Comstock

Au Privave
(No. 2)

By Charlie Parker

VERVE 8010/VERVE 8840/VERVE 8002

Chi Chi

By Charlie Parker

VERVE 8005/MGM 4949/VERVE 8409

(TURN PAGE)

Chi Chi – cont.

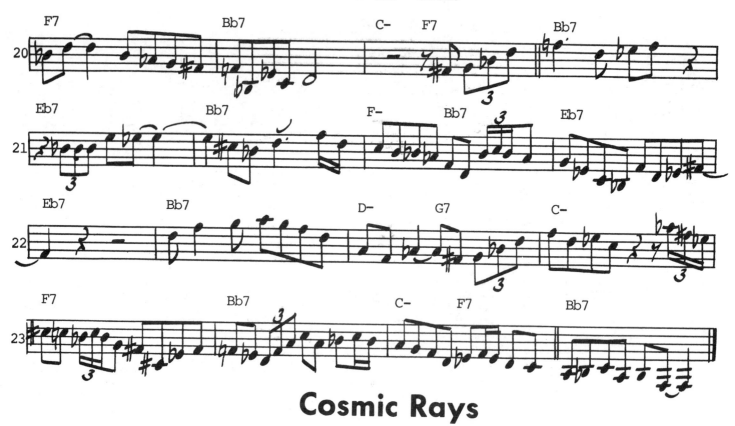

Cosmic Rays

By Charlie Parker

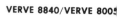

VERVE 8840/VERVE 800⁵

Cosmic Rays - cont.

Laird Baird

By Charlie Parker

VERVE 8005

33

She Rote
(No. 1)

By Charlie Parker

VERVE 8010/VERVE 8840/VERVE 8002/VERVE 2515

She Rote

(No. 2)

By Charlie Parker

VERVE 8010/MGM 4949

Mohawk
(No. 1)

By Charlie Parker

VERVE 8006/VERVE 8840/VERVE 2501

Mohawk
(No. 2)

By Charlie Parker

VERVE 8006/VERVE 8002

An Oscar For Treadwell

By Charlie Parker

VERVE 8002/VERVE 8006/VERVE 2501

(Turn Page)

Constellation

By Charlie Parker

SAVOY 2201

(Turn Page)

Constellation - cont.

Polynesian

Criterion's Book 1
HAWAIIAN SONG BOOK
FOR PIANO, GUITAR & VOICE

Complete words and music to 26 Hawaiian hit songs. Featuring PEARLY SHELLS, FOREVERMORE, MAPUANA, VINI VINI, NO HUHU, I'LL SEE YOU IN HAWAII, etc.

Criterion's Book 2
ISLAND SONG BOOK
FOR PIANO, GUITAR & VOICE

Complete words and music to 31 Hawaiian hit songs. Featuring TINY BUBBLES, E MALIU MAI (Hawaiian Love Call), KAINOA, There Goes KEALOHA, SINGING BAMBOO, THAT'S THE HAWAIIAN IN ME, etc.

Criterion's Authentic
HAWAIIAN BOOK FOR ALL ORGANS
(With registrations for Pipe, Electric and Pre-Set Organs)

Complete words and music to 17 Hawaiian hit songs, including PEARLY SHELLS, QUIET VILLAGE, FAREWELL, NO HUHU, WAIKIKI, MAPUANA, etc.

Criterion's
EXOTIC BOOK FOR ALL ORGANS
(With registrations for Pipe, Electric and Pre-Set Organs)

Words & music and instrumentals of 15 Exotic Hit songs, including QUIET VILLAGE; MOUNTAIN HIGH, VALLEY LOW; OFF SHORE; SONG OF INDIA; HOUSE OF BAMBOO, etc.

SOUTH SEA FOLIOS
Songs from Hawaii, Tahiti, Samoa & Maori

Book #1 — SOUTH SEA SONGS
Book #2 — SONGS OF POLYNESIA
Book #3 — ISLAND SONGS
Book #4 — MAORI MELODIES
Book #5 — SONGS OF PARADISE
Book #6 — SONGS FROM THE PACIFIC ISLES
Book #7 — SONGS FROM THE ROMANTIC ISLANDS
Book #8 — TUNES FROM THE TROPICS

Contains words and music for voice and all single note instruments—ukulele, guitar, etc. . . .

CRITERION'S HAWAIIAN SING-A-SONG LYRIC BOOK
Words to 84 Hawaiian favorites New & Old
Includes TINY BUBBLES, PEARLY SHELLS, OFF SHORE, QUIET VILLAGE, etc.

Donna Lee

By Charlie Parker

SAVOY 2201

2ND CHORUS

3rd CHORUS

(Turn Page)

Donna Lee – cont.

Kim
(No. 1)

By Charlie Parker

VERVE 8005/VERVE 8840

(Turn Page)

Kim (No. 1) – cont.

ORCHESTRATIONS

SMALL ORCHESTRATIONS

MODERN SOUND SERIES
Charlie Parker's
CONFIRMATION — YARDBIRD SUITE
MOOSE THE MOOCHE — ORNITHOLOGY
SCRAPPLE FROM THE APPLE
DEWEY SQUARE

Gerry Mulligan's MULLIGANETTES
BERNIE'S TUNE — WALKIN' SHOES
NIGHTS AT THE TURNTABLE —
SOFT SHOE — FREEWAY

Illinois Jacquet's
ROBBINS' NEST
Coleman Hawkin's
STUFFY
Lester Young's
JUMPIN' WITH SYMPHONY SID

Dizzy Gillespie's
THE CHAMP

STANDARD DANCE ORCHESTRATIONS

AUTUMN CONCERTO
(My Heart Reminds Me)
BERNIE'S TUNE
DREAM
INTERMISSION RIFF
IT'S A GOOD DAY

MARINA
MOONLIGHT IN VERMONT
OFF SHORE
QUIET VILLAGE
(AT) THE END (OF A
RAINBOW)

QUANDO LA LUNA (Small orch.)

Kim
(No. 2)

By Charlie Parker

VERVE 8005/MGM 4949

(Turn Page)

Kim (No. 2) – cont.

Cheryl

By Charlie Parker

SAVOY 1108

GUITAR

GUITAR FOLIOS

"BOOTS" FOR GUITAR
Guitar arrangements with complete parts for Solo and Rhythm Guitar . . . . .

FROM THE ROMANTIC ERA
Concert guitar solos transcribed from Laurindo Almeida's Capitol album, music of Beethoven, Greig, etc . . . . .

BOSSA GUITARRA
Six solos by Laurindo Almeida with lead line and chord symbols . . . .

SURFIN' GUITAR
Surfing songs arranged by Jimmie Haskell for piano solo and guitar solo . . . . .

COUNTRY GUITAR
Hits from the Country Field . . . .

FOLKSY SONGS FOR GUITAR (Simple to Advanced)
"MTA", "Philadelphia Lawyer", etc . . . .

20 GREAT TUNES FOR GUITAR (Pick Style)
39 Great Arrangements by Dan Fox, featuring "Moonlight In Vermont" . . . .

OSCAR MOORE GUITAR SOLOS
. . . .

VENTURE FOLIOS

Book #1 — Hits like WALK DON'T RUN
Book #2 — Hits like JOURNEY TO THE STARS
Book #3 — Hits like JOSE, INSTANT GUITARS
Book #4 — Hits like DIAMOND HEAD, GRINGO

GUITAR SOLOS

AMOR FLAMENCO
BAJA
BODACIOUS & ANGRY GENERATION
BULLERIAS Y CANCION
TEHUACAN

. . . .

GUITAR BOOKS

GUITAR TUTOR by Laurindo Almeida
A complete Concert Guitar Method . . . . .

THE GUITAR by Barney Kessell
A unique guide for guitarists . . . .

Thriving From A Riff

By Charlie Parker

SAVOY 2201

Ko Ko

By Charlie Parker

SAVOY 2201

(Turn Page)

Ko Ko - cont.

Red Cross

By Charlie Parker

SAVOY 2201

Marmaduke

By Charlie Parker

SAVOY 2201

(Turn Page)

Marmaduke - cont.

Barbados

By Charlie Parker

SAVOY 1108

SHAPING FORCES IN MUSIC

By Ernst Toch

An inquiry into harmony, melody, counterpoint and form. A complete advanced music course now being used by many leading colleges as their text book.

Perhaps

By Charlie Parker

SAVOY 2201

Now's The Time
(No. 1)

By Charlie Parker

VERVE 8840

BLUES ♩=132

For Melody see Now's The Time (No. 2) - page 76

UNDERSCORE

By Frank Skinner

A complete course in scoring for motion pictures and television, featuring an
actual score that was writtern, arranged and recorded for a motion picture, with
timing sheets, orchestra sketches and orchestrations.

Now's The Time
(No. 2)

By Charlie Parker

SAVOY 2201

Buzzy

By Charlie Parker

SAVOY 2201

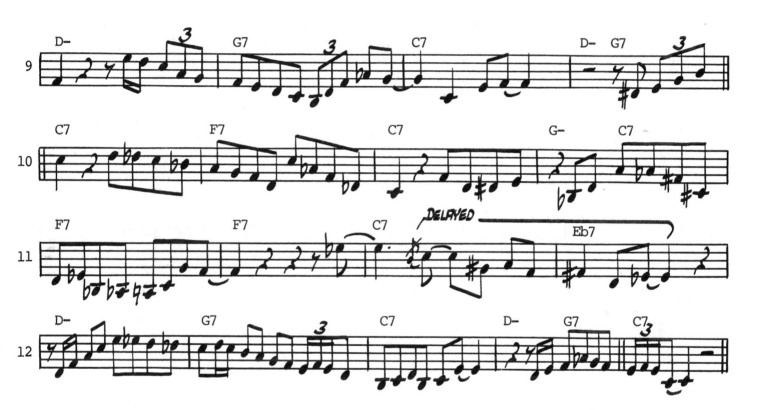

Billie's Bounce

(also known as BILL'S BOUNCE)

By Charlie Parker

SAVOY 2201

Chasing The Bird

By Charlie Parker

SAVOY 1108

Blue Bird

By Charlie Parker

SAVOY 2201

Ah-Leu-Cha
(also known as AH LEV CHA)

By Charlie Parker

SAVOY 2201

(Turn Page)

Ah-Leu-Cha - cont.

Klaun Stance

By Charlie Parker

SAVOY 2201

(Turn Page)

Klaun. - cont.

Card Board

By Charlie Parker

VERVE 2501

W.W.

Bird Gets The Worm

By Charlie Parker

SAVOY 2201

(Turn Page)

Bird Gets The Worm - cont.

Segment

By Charlie Parker

VERVE 8009

(Turn Page)

W.W.

98

Segment – cont.

Visa

By Charlie Parker

VERVE 8000/VERVE 8009

Passport

By Charlie Parker

VERVE 8000/VERVE 8009

W.W.

Another Hairdo

By Charlie Parker

SAVOY 2201

Back Home Blues

By Charlie Parker

VERVE 8840/VERVE 8000/VERVE 8010/VERVE 2515

W.W.

Bloomdido

By Charlie Parker

VERVE 8840/MGM 4949/VERVE 8006/VERVE 2501

The Bird

By Charlie Parker

VERVE 2501

W.W.

Steeplechase

By Charlie Parker

SAVOY 2201

Diverse

By Charlie Parker

VERVE 8009

(Turn Page)

Diverse – cont.

Merry-Go-Round

By Charlie Parker

SAVOY 2201

(Turn Page)

Merry-Go-Round - cont.

My Little Suede Shoes

By Charlie Parker

VERVE 8000/VERVE 2515

Relaxing With Lee

By Charlie Parker

VERVE 8840/VERVE 8009/VERVE 2501

Blues (Fast)

By Charlie Parker

VERVE 8840/VERVE 8009/VERVE 250

W.W.

124

(Turn Page)

Blues (Fast) – cont.

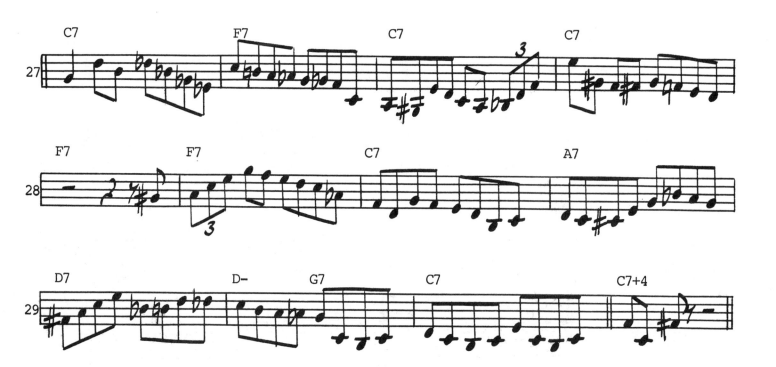

CRITERION'S BOOKS & JAZZ PUBLICATIONS

FIRST CHART by Van Alexander (Edited and
  Contributed to by Jimmy Haskell)
An important elementary arranging book. Features step-by-step instruction to help musicians through that "first chart." Includes all the modern styles, Jazz-Rock, Blues-Rock, Contemporary Latin, etc. Includes a record of two of the charts including John C. Fogerty hit for Credence Clearwater Revival, "Lookin' Out My Back Door". 112 pp.   **Price $14.95**

THE PROFESSIONAL ARRANGER COMPOSER
  (Book One) by Russ Garcia
Text book used by leading schools. Basis for course for practical arranging and composing in the commercial field. For the advanced and professional arranger. 172 pp., 1951   **Price $14.95**

THE PROFESSIONAL ARRANGER COMPOSER
  (Book Two) by Russ Garcia
Discusses contemporary trends in Jazz, Pop and "Modern Classical" Techniques. New scales, chords etc. using tone rows in practical music. Contains a record of many of the 169 examples and the recording of a complete score of a composition by Garcia. 91 pp., 1978   **Price $14.95**

NEW HOT DISCOGRAPHY by Charles Delaunay
The standard directory of recorded jazz. Titles, personnel, dates and numbers of 20,000 records. 608 pp.   **Price $24.95**

THE STECHESON CLASSIFIED SONG
  DIRECTORY by Anne & Anthony Stecheson
A classified directory of over 100,000 song titles, 395 different categories. Used by every major record company. 503 pp.
incl. 68 pg. supplement   **Price $40.00**

CHARLIE PARKER OMNIBOOK
60 Recorded Solos — 4 Books
Eb...C...Bb...Bass Clef *(New!)*
Price $11.95

New! **CHARLIE PARKER FOR PIANO**
15 Piano Solos Based on His Recordings
Arranged by Paul Smith and Morris Feldman
Price $7.95

CHARLIE PARKER FOR PIANO
Recorded by The Paul Smith Trio
Cassettes available **$8.98** by mail

CRITERION MUSIC CORPORATION
6124 Selma Avenue, Hollywood, CA 90028

Shawnuff

By Charlie Parker and John 'Dizzy' Gillespie

PHOENIX 17
JAZZ

(Turn Page)

Leap Frog

By Charlie Parker

VERVE 8840/VERVE 8002/VERVE 8006/VERVE 2501

W.W.

Leap Frog - cont.

(Turn Page)

Leap Frog - cont.

Parker's Mood

By Charlie Parker

SAVOY SJL2201

Warming Up A Riff

By Charlie Parker

SAVOY SJL2201

(Turn Page)

Si Si

By Charlie Parker

VERVE VE2-2512

CHARLIE PARKER FOR PIANO
Recorded by The Paul Smith Trio
Cassettes available $8.98 by mail

CRITERION MUSIC CORPORATION
6124 Selma Avenue, Hollywood, CA 90028

141

Ballade

By Charlie Parker

VERVE MGV8002